Advan

Unshakeable PEACE

Unshakable Peace—the title alone is captivating. When a person reflects on their life and things they have conquered to experience unshakable peace is powerful. Latifa takes us on a journey throughout her life, not just to tell a story but to bring awareness to what other young girls and women may have experienced.

    Unshakable Peace is full of joy, pain, triumph, love, hurt, reflection, revelation but most of all it is filled with the heart of Latifa's journey.

-Maisha Howze, Author of *W.A.S.H.: Withstand all Strife to Heal* and *Hidden Gems: Black Women in the Workplace*

What God has given Latifa will catapult you into walking courageously out of perfection, being voiceless, feeling unprotected, and trying to find your place in a world that pretends you don't exist.

Unshakeable Peace will encourage you to know that you are not alone in the challenges you face along your journey. This book gives you permission to embrace the power that is within you to impact the world.

- LaDina Strawder, Author of *Killing Grace: A Rise to Restoration* and *Love Wins: Nikki's Tale*

While reading *Unshakeable Peace*, I realized I've been just existing my whole life. I don't want to just exist, I want to live in purpose, on purpose.

Charmaine Harris, Owner
Anchored to Detail

Unshakeable PEACE

Unshakeable PEACE

BREAK OUT OF SHAME, DISCOVER YOUR WORTH AND FIND YOUR PEACE

LATIFA MILLER

Unshakeable Peace: Break out of Shame, Discover Your Worth and Find Your Peace

Copyright © 2023 by Latifa Miller

ISBN: 979-8-218-12414-4

Published by: Daughters of Zion Communications
Printed in the United States of America

Internal Layout and Design: InSCRIBEd Inspiration, LLC.

Edited by: La Dina Anderson, Maisha Howze, Charmaine
         Harris, Penda L. James & Latifa Miller

Cover Art: Soleil Branding Essentials
www.soleilbrandingessentials.com

All real-life anecdotes are told with permission from actual parties involved and recorded to the best of the author's recollection. Names in some instances have not been used at the request of the individuals referenced. In some cases, parties mentioned are deceased. Details of some instances have been slightly modified to enhance readability, or to ensure privacy. Any resemblance of any other parties is purely coincidental.

TRIGGER WARNING: Please be advised that *Unshakeable Peace* contains subject matter that may be upsetting to some readers. It contains a scenario of sexual assault.

DEDICATION

This book is dedicated to my mother Ruth O. Davis. I am because of her sacrifice and I stand on her shoulders.

I also dedicate this book to my paternal grandparents Percy L. and Naomi C. Davis. I was the apple of their eye. They taught me unconditional love, laughter, and the value of being my authentic self. I am grateful they loved me while believing God's best for my life.

CONTENTS

Contents

PRELUDE – STRONG BLACK WOMEN

I grew up on Rugby Street in Philadelphia, Pennsylvania. WDAS 105.3 FM radio station played on the surround sound stereo system at my mom's house, and it was the backdrop to my childhood. I played outside until the first streetlight came on and drank water from the water hose. I played double Dutch and walked to the store for penny candy. Posters of my favorite boy bands were on my walls, and I made three-way calls to discuss my biggest secrets.

In the summer there were block parties and as kids, we weren't too cool to play in the fire hydrant. On Friday nights my friends and I got rides to the roller rink and on Sundays we walked to the movie theater.

I was raised by strong Black women who blazed the trail so that I could exist. Growing up in the 70's I admired the strength and fight of the women in my life, yet some of what they modeled did not produce the fruit that they deserved. I saw brokenness in the women who surrounded me—my aunts, cousins, and neighbors were strong and capable, yet they were unable to find the strength to walk in their purpose. None of the women in my life had been where I was trying to go.

> *"A woman*
> *needs her soul*
> *to be whole*
> *in order to thrive."*
>
> ~Latifa Miller

Looking back, I see that I was always different, some would say, "set apart." While the women I looked up to were too torn down by life to figure it out, I was optimistic. They were too tired to fight for what they wanted, and I chased my dreams. I recognized that by the time I came of age, the strong women in my life were exhausted from their own battles. They had already given their all to survive and when I would experience something difficult, I would think of them and ask myself, *"Is this enough? Am I going to be enough?"* As I grew into womanhood, I became what some of them didn't know how to: compassionate, loving, and sensual.

Watching the women in my life showed me how broken women breed broken little girls who grow up missing the tools they need to become whole. I believe that Black women need their souls to be whole to thrive. I needed the women in my life to be strong so I could thrive. What I learned as I became a woman is that those women blazed the trail so that I could stand in my power. They were strong and I stand on their shoulders. When I stand in my power, I extend the grace to make space for others to stand in their power, also.

It took time, faith, and intentionality, but I found my *Unshakeable Peace.* In this book I have opened my heart with my narrative which includes poetry and some of my favorite affirmations. I hope this book will help you believe that you are enough, and that this belief will strengthen your resolve.

~Latifa

Part I – Break Out of Shame

Unshakeable

Unshakeable PEACE

"*I am the daughter of Ruth.*
Ruth is the daughter of Lena.

Lena is the daughter of Ella.
I am because of them."

~Latifa Miller

A RUTH AND A NAOMI

In the bible the book of Ruth is about a woman who sat at the feet of her mother-in-law Naomi to be taught, groomed, and ushered into her divine purpose. Naomi's instructions and guidance saved Ruth. Ruth's obedience to those instructions saved them both. In my life I needed both a Ruth and a Naomi to mold me into the woman I would become. They each played critical roles in teaching me the importance of womanhood. Between my mother Ruth, and my Grandmom, Naomi, I was blessed and well cared for. God was intentional when He gave me a Ruth and a Naomi to shape my life.

Naomi

Naomi was my paternal Grandmom, and she showed me God through her eyes. Grandmom was a nurturer and a woman of faith. She was an evangelist and taught me about grace and unconditional love. Naomi was gentle, kind, and nurturing. She loved me and poured her best into me including her faith. Grandmom took me to Sunday school and Vacation Bible School; because of her, I knew God was real, long before I knew Him personally.

Grandmom and I would take walks in the fields by her house in South Jersey. We picked wildflowers. Her laughter was contagious, and her joy is etched into my memory. Little did I know these memories would sustain me when my world was falling apart. When I would smile outwardly while crumbling on the inside, I remembered my joy in life and my Grandmom's faith. I learned how to worship and believe God because of my Grandmom.

While my mother was resistant to my Grandmom's teaching and covering for her life, thankfully, my Grandmom persisted in her attempts to teach me valuable life lessons. My mother kept the door open for Naomi to teach me. When my mother could not pour into me, Grandmom transferred everything I needed spiritually and emotionally. Grandmom was my safety, my protection, my peace, and my guide. I ultimately held onto her wisdom in tough situations. I was her Ruth.

My mom wasn't a churchgoer, in fact she kept her distance due to church hurt. Nevertheless, she always packed my Sundays best when I went to Grandmom's for the weekend. When I got older, Grandmom traveled from South Jersey to Philly to take me to Sunday School at a church around the corner from our house. My mother would get me up early and dressed up in my Sunday best and Grandmom would miss her own church service just to drive me to a church near my house. Grandmom had no connection to the congregation, but she knew they were believers who offered Sunday school to a brown girl like me.

Ruth

I am the best part of my mom. She sacrificed so much to allow me to have the life of her dreams. At a young age she understood that education was an opportunity for a person to excel and she pressed the importance of education into me. Today, I am the manifestation of those dreams.

My mother is the youngest of a sharecropper. During harvest time she hid in the fields when the school bus drove by because she didn't want the other kids to know she had to go to work. Ruth was my provider. She kept me clothed, fed, and educated.

My mom's hustle kept me in private school, the lights and heat were never compromised, and we always had a car to get where we needed to be. I had nice clothes and appropriate shoes. I had popular toys, games including ColecoVision® and a 13" television in my room. Almost 40 years later, I came across an ad about the best toys from the 80's and I recognized each one of them because I had most of them.

I also had amazing opportunities such as traveling to Spain for Spanish class. I will never know the price, or the sacrifice that my mother had to make to give me what she valued.

I played the piano. I even had a baby grand in my mother's living room. I was in the choir, but I didn't consider myself a musician or an artist. I attended a private school, but I struggled to thrive academically.

I had a lot, but not always what I thought that I needed. I grew up with voids that resulted in gaping holes in my life because I spent a lot of time alone. I needed to be loved differently. Because I had things and seemed better off than others, most people didn't notice me, the voiceless, brown-skinned girl with an aching heart.

That's what happened to me living in the middle. I was in between, not really this, and not really that. I could not identify with or relate to most of the things or people who surrounded me because I was stuck.

I wanted to make my mother proud of me. At one time she did say that I was a horrible person. Even though we misunderstood each other, struggled to bond, and never had a deep connection like other mothers and daughters, our love was deep, true, and everlasting.

I am because of my mother.

Gratitude

I am grateful
I am not ashamed of my truth
I am loved
I am unique
I maintain my peace
I am worthy
I am not mediocre
I will speak up even through the tears.
I am valuable just as I am
I am my own priority
I will shine even in the rain
I am light
I am uniquely made and set apart
I am intelligent
I matter
I am called, needed and full of purpose
I am full of compassion
I am supported
I am anointed
I walk in purpose
I am a world changer
I am my sister's keeper
I am lovable
I am complex
I am sensible
I am reliable
I am equipped
I am creative
I am capable

I am knowledgeable
I am passionate
I am a teacher
I am student
I am loyal, loving, and full of life
I am articulate, affectionate and attentive
I am thoughtful
I am inspiring and inspirational
I am faithful & fabulous
I am an advocate & ambitious
I am relentless

Unshakeable
PEACE

*"My life becomes different
as I grow."*

~Latifa Miller

Set Up for Success

What you do today sets you up for success
tomorrow
It is critical that you don't take days for
granted
Remember that you should be taking steps to
move yourself forward
Don't get stuck in the past
Don't allow the twists and turns of life to hold
you back from believing that you can succeed
Success is in your future
You are capable and you have what you need
to do it
Go ahead and
put your best foot forward
Make the best of today and go for it

EARLY SCHOOL YEARS

Before starting half-day preschool at House of Prayer, I went to a home-based daycare around the corner from my mom's job. I specifically remember arriving just as the theme music for the babysitter's soap opera came on and the other children would be napping. I don't have many memories from House of Prayer, but there is one that stands out to me. I remember standing in line to see Santa to get a wrapped gift for Christmas.

In typical fashion, we stood in height order, and I was the last in line. Just before my turn, they ran out of toys. I stood alone waiting as they tried to find something to give me. It felt like an eternity, and I wanted Santa to find something for me. Finally, someone brought me an unwrapped toy that was found in the infant room.

It occurred to me that if I'd been shorter, I would not have been the one standing without a present. At that young age, probably around three or four, I had already begun to question my place and value in the community where I lived.

The following year I started kindergarten at a black Christian school. My Mom's coworker had referred her to the newly established school. Most of the students were black as well as our principal.

On the first day when I met my teacher, I thought about how short she was. As tall as I stood, with legs for days, we were almost eye-to-eye.

I think we had fun and I guess we learned a lot since we matriculated to first grade. My first-grade teacher, Ms. Steward, was an older black woman. She was rigid and gave us assigned seats. She would shake her ruler at us when she talked. Ms. Steward was smart and soft like my grandmom. I remember having homework every day in first grade.

I also remember a boy who sat in the back of the class and whispered girl's names. When I would turn around, he would expose himself to me. No one ever talked about that. In first grade, I learned how to work hard and how to keep secrets.

Fourth grade is more memorable than second and third grade. We were the oldest students in the elementary school building, so the adults were always teaching our class the importance of independence and leadership.

Miss Hollinger, our teacher, taught us random presidential and political facts and she ran mock elections to help us learn. Jimmy Carter was running for reelection against Ronald Reagan.

I had my first argument that year. During break I noticed that my water cup was missing. The popular girls were giggling, and the cute boys were mocking me asking, "Who has your cup Latifa?"

I felt vulnerable. The teacher acted like it wasn't a big deal, but it was. I saw my cup on the desk of the girl who always yanked my ponytails, so I took it back. Apparently, my approach was too aggressive, and the girl made a big deal of it. I got in trouble for taking my cup back. The teacher told me, "You should have politely asked her for it."

> *"Never settle.*
> *Everything that settles*
> *is at the bottom."*
>
> ~Heath Bailey

As I listened to my reprimand, I wondered why no one advised her not to take things that didn't belong to her. I knew for sure my mom would not be replacing my cup for the remainder of the year. She would say that because I was irresponsible, I did not deserve a new cup, especially since she was on a tight budget.

Why didn't anyone tell the other students not to laugh at a student in distress? That experience taught me the power of popularity.

Later that year I got in trouble for kicking a boy between his legs. Our classroom was on an upper level of the school. We were lined up in height order to go to the cafeteria. I was at the end of the line with another girl. As we snaked our way down the staircase, the boys in the front of the line found it funny to try to look up our dresses. I did not find the humor in it.

When we got to the cafeteria, a few boys whispered, "I saw your undies."

I told the lunch lady and she said, "It's just boys being boys."

I later told a teacher, and she told me, "Don't worry. There was no way they could actually see up your dress from their angle."

On the bus, I told a couple of boys I knew, my mom's coworker's sons. They were in the middle school building, and they threatened the boys to stop. One of them said, "If the boys keep doing it, fight back."

Nothing seemed to sway those boys and their relentless behavior. I felt vulnerable, again because they would not stop. One weekend my big cousin E told me, "Kick him in the nuts."

I didn't even know what "nuts" were, or where they were, but he showed me exactly what to do, and I did it the next time one of the boys taunted us. After it happened, I got called to the office. The principal said, "Your actions could damage their manhood." Then the principal turned to my mom and said, "Her aggressive behavior is problematic."

At that age I was beginning to see a pattern of defeat. Fourth grade was my last year at that school and Jimmy Carter lost the mock election, too.

THE MIDDLE

I felt insignificant and forgettable growing up. I was not sure if I mattered or if I would have the influence that was going to change the world. I wasn't sure if I cared, though. I often referred to myself as a piece of "wallpaper" because I preferred to just disappear into the background.

No one asked if I needed anything. I hoped someone would take a deeper look into my eyes and see the void. I had become voiceless in the crowd.

If I made a mistake, everybody made a fuss about it. When I did things right it went unnoticed so I would embellish stories to make them as good as possible to avoid criticism.

Eventually, I found myself doing things because I was seeking positive attention. I was consumed with trying to find the balance between staying off the radar of criticism while being affirmed for who I was, not who they thought I should be. With all the opportunities I was afforded, there was potential to be great, but I was just mediocre. I was always in the middle and—just not quite enough to matter.

I wasn't failing any of my classes, yet I was not getting good grades either. I didn't live in the projects, but we were far from living in the suburbs with the fancy houses. The folks still in the ghettos thought we had moved on up and made it, but the affluent made sure to let us know we did not belong with their kind.

My complexion was brown. I wasn't light enough to pass for white, or dark enough to be called out of my name. I wasn't poor and did not miss any meals, but I wasn't rich, and I didn't have the luxury of choice. I ate what was given to me and most times the option was egg salad sandwiches.

While I towed the line in the middle as an average kid, outsiders perceived I had no worries since I wasn't dealing with an extreme or distress of any kind. The middle was a heavy load for me to balance, and it never served me well. I was not sure how to tap into my potential.

MY DAD

I was raised in the maze of my parents'
imperfections. I knew my dad and his family,
but I was not raised in a two-parent home. I
knew my father's presence and I wasn't
neglected. In fact, a distant cousin learned a
few years ago that my parents were never
married. Seeing us function as a family unit
by attending weddings, funerals, and
reunions it appeared that they were together
and intact. In reality, my father's nick name,
"Round a Bout" had some truth to it.

People have told me that my dad broke my
mom's heart when I was five-years-old and
that she never got over it. In spite of that,
they managed to coparent me without parting
ways. My mom tells me that my daddy wasn't
around much, yet I remember him being
there for me.

I remember my dad being there in
kindergarten when the driver let me off at the
wrong bus stop and I had to find my way
home. In middle school, I remember him
building my Barbie Dream house on
Christmas Eve. He taught me how to drive too
and I passed my driver's test on the first try.

In eleventh grade, my father picked me up from school when I sprained my ankle after falling on the steps. It was my first event, and I was preparing to welcome a guest speaker as president of the newly formed Black Action Society. I was nervous and excited at the huge opportunity but instead of shining in the moment, I was in the front office holding ice on my ankle waiting on a ride to the Emergency Room. My dad sensed that I was feeling ashamed and defeated; he took me for ice cream.

My father was there for me. He was present for each milestone birthday party and every graduation.

A Surprise Change

During my sophomore year of college, my mom found love again, married, and planned to relocate to Florida. I knew that she was excited, yet nervous about the change. I wanted her to be happy and was excited for the next phase of her journey.

I had no idea the impact that this change would have on my life. My mom took a few months to get her affairs in order before the move. That summer, I had planned to pack up my things and prepare for the transition over break. However, when I returned from a short 10-day visit with my cousins in

California I discovered that my mom had moved. I was jarred because the home I knew was gone.

I was told that my parents had argued a lot while I was gone. Word on the street was that Daddy was jealous and wanted my mom back. Again, that was baffling to me, and I tried to stay out of it. Honestly, I didn't understand why they had never settled down, but they seemed to manage their arrangement without a commitment.

When I returned to my childhood home there was only a box of beautiful prom dresses that were handmade for me by mom, Aunt Mae, and Aunt Selena. My sweet sixteen dress was in the box, too. I was hopeful the rest of my things would be in the new home. However, when I arrived at the new home in Florida, I discovered that most of my valued belongings were missing.

I only kept the sweet sixteen dress from that box. My mom later said, "Your bedroom furniture and my living room furniture are in storage. You can get them when you are ready for your first place." That brought me peace because my grandparents gifted me the bedroom furniture as a little girl.

When I returned to Philly to prepare to go back to school, my dad took me to two storage units. As he rolled up the gate I saw my things and so many of my childhood memories. Apparently, while many people thought my parents' arguments were about him being, "a day late and a dollar short" in his efforts to win my mom back, the arguments were about her choices.

As she was cleaning out the house, he was digging through the "trash" retrieving my belongings and things he thought I may want to keep. He hadn't been there day to day in my life and didn't know what I would feel was valuable, so he grabbed her cast iron frying pan, a painting I made in sixth grade art class that had been in an art show and a poem my friend, "Big O" had written me in high school about his perception of me that was in the bottom of my jewelry box. His poem talked about the fullness of my lips and the power of my walk. His words jumped off the page and made me feel seen.

"Big O" reminded me of my worth, power and sensuality. I remembered the words of his poem whenever I talked to a guy. While I was glad to have the letter back, I hoped that neither of my parents had read it or my diaries. It turns out that my dad was looking out for me.

At that age, I felt both abandoned and seen. It was a complex time.

Growing Up and Growing Into Myself

Growing up and growing into myself
　　I wondered if I mattered

Growing up and growing into myself
I was missing out on joy because I locked the
　　　　　door.
I did it to keep the bad out, but then the good
couldn't get in. I had to learn to protect my
emotions differently and figure out a way to
　　　manage things differently.

Growing up and growing into myself
I am learning to stop worrying about the
mistakes of my childhood and understanding
　　that they will partner with my past.
I am learning to allow them to shape my path
　　and add power and presence to my
　　　　　purpose.

Growing up and growing into myself
I have learned that leading with wisdom
means being right isn't always necessary.

Growing up and growing into myself
　　I felt discounted and dismissed.
I hate that I still struggle with that.
I know it's not true, but it feels like it.
　　　　I measured my worth
　　　by how people treated me.

When I was overlooked, left behind,
unnurtured and unheard
I questioned my worth.

When I was raped, I questioned my worth.
I didn't say anything to protect our
indiscretions
I didn't say anything to protect him
It stayed with me no matter how hard I said,
I am enough
I still wonder.

Growing up and growing into myself
I struggled. I didn't know my place.
I never fit in. Then or now.
Who was I protecting?
When Dad wasn't around, I didn't complain
because I wanted to protect his image
When Dad made memories with other
families, I didn't share my hurt because I
wanted to protect little me

When My mom's sacrifice felt like neglect, I
tried to suck it up because I wanted to
protect her

I am ENOUGH
I am ENOUGH
I am ENOUGH
I am ENOUGH
I am ENOUGH

Latifa is Enough

I am ENOUGH in spite of my mistakes and
transgressions
I am ENOUGH

BLACK GIRL IN AN ALL-WHITE SCHOOL

In fifth grade I transferred to an all-girls school. Fifth grade was a hard year for me emotionally. Going to the new school required me to become a "latchkey kid," which wasn't uncommon in the eighties. When I got home from school, I would let myself in and stay in the house until my mom got home from work. I remember having a nightmare that caused me to fear staying at home alone.

In the nightmare, I could see through my window that someone was breaking in the back door. I couldn't stop them from getting in the house. It felt like I couldn't run or escape, so I hid in a corner. I remember feeling myself freeze in the nightmare because I did not want to be seen by the burglar. I would awaken from the nightmare panting in fear just as the burglar was about to find my hiding space.

That dream felt real. It stayed with me for months, keeping me frozen in fear. I confided in my mom, but she just kept telling me, "You'll be fine. No one is going to break in the house."

I didn't feel fine. I was powerless, scared, and anxious. I was a kid who felt alone and afraid. Her words did not comfort me or make me feel secure at home alone. I wanted and needed protection from my mom. I thought asking for help would be a solution, but I had to figure things out for myself.

To help me face my fears, Grandmom reminded me to sing a song to God for comfort. I made one up that was written in my heart, and I found peace humming the words to myself, "Jesus, help us to do what's right and lead us on our way, Lead us on our wayyyyyyy." I didn't know at the time that I was a songwriter. God had given me a gift in those words, and I sang them every time I was alone, afraid, and unsure. Those words carried me through many dark days and times of uncertainty.

A lot of things begin to change for me mentally when I was a latch key kid. I became stronger by pretending that everything was always good. Mind over matter got me through most things. I'll never know how fear entered my life in that dream. Looking back, I wonder what was happening in my subconscious mind that made me have that kind of bad dream. I didn't watch scary or science fiction movies.

I know that asking for help and not getting it from my mom contributed to my feeling of voicelessness. Feeling unsupported by my mother during my formative years was foundational in my development and it took me a long while to break through that mindset.

I still sing the song I wrote as a child for comfort. Don't be surprised if you ever hear me singing, "Jesus, help us to do what's right and lead us on our way, Lead us on our wayyyyyyy."

School Blues

I remember the big driveway in front of the school had a huge Sweetgum tree in the middle. The botanical name was "Liquidambar." I learned the proper name in sixth-grade science when we had to adopt a tree and learn about the scientific background.

My mom registered me for the all-white gender-specific school on faith—she did not have the means to cover the cost. I wasn't prepared for the culture shock that transitioning from an all-black, co-ed school would bring. The girls there wore uniform skirts and there was assigned seating in every class. In my former school, we wore uniforms, but we sat wherever we landed. The teachers were pleased to get a much-needed break from us.

In my previous schools the cafeteria and gym were in the same space. We would put the lunch tables away to have gym class. Our library was a set of bookshelves in the back of the classroom, and the science lab was the teacher's desk.

The new school had a gym with lines painted on the floor and basketball rims. The library had double doors, reading nooks, and a full-time librarian and the science room had lab tables for students to do their own experiments. It was massive.

We had lockers, carpet, and central air conditioning. The school had two libraries and a separate gym and cafeteria. All of these amenities were indicators of the quality of education I was going to receive at my new school.

I immediately failed my French class. Most of the students had taken French classes for four years; it was an advanced class. Before my second term, it was decided I was no longer required to take French and was given the option to take a different elective.

At this new school there were two different math classes, two different English classes, and did I mention, almost everyone was White. I didn't believe I was smart enough for the school. As it turned out, I was given favor to remain in the school. I actually failed my admissions test and we couldn't meet the financial requirements, yet I was granted admission.

My mom paid what she could when she could. I remember regularly being called to the office and asked to hand deliver letters to my mom. I didn't know they were delinquency letters, but the next day she would tell me, "Put on your best sweater, and put those pretty ribbons in your hair." She sent me to school anyway. Time and time again my mom stood on her hope and determination.

Eventually, they sent another letter explaining that they found an alumna who was willing to cover my tuition for the rest of the year. My tuition was going to be reviewed each year until I graduated. Each year, I was awarded a scholarship. Good is good!

Recently my dad mailed me a box of pictures he found after my grandmother passed and in the box was a copy of the original letter stating that I had an anonymous alumnae to cover my tuition. (Thanks Daddy for keeping that letter!)

The Low Track

The school had different classes for different learning levels. Due to my skill level in grammar, English, and math, I was placed in the low English and math tracks. By seventh grade, my math teacher realized I could do high-level math but moving me to the advanced math class wasn't allowed because I was on the low track.

Mrs. Bakewell didn't push back on the policy, yet she moved my seat near her desk in the front of the class. Moving seats was uncommon and I thought I was in trouble at first, but she gave me "special" math packets to complete.

Mrs. Bakewell gave me high-level math work and graded me accordingly. At the end of eight grade, she had me test out of ninth-grade math and forced the administrators to place me on the math fast track. Mrs. Bakewell was a great teacher who strategically used her influence to help me. When she retired, she was the head of the math department.

Years later, I Googled her and learned she died. I reached out to her daughters on social media and shared with them the impact their mom had on my life when she was my teacher. She challenged authority in a meaningful way on my behalf and I am forever grateful.

These classroom experiences became my Ground Zero for lessons I learned about injustice and advocacy. Because Mrs. Bakewell modeled how to help others navigate through uncomfortable spaces without waiting for permission, she moved in her area of control to make meaningful change. I seek justice for students who are hiding in plain sight like I was.

I was a good girl in high school. I was confident and a peacemaker amongst my peers. I had a friend named Dee who wrote a poem about my gifts, strengths, and best attributes. He presented it to me as a framed gift and I hung it on my wall. Those beautiful words gave me joy.

Gatekeepers and Role Models

As a child, I hated it when the neighborhood watch lady always told on me if I took a risk or broke a rule. I realize now that she saw my value and took the time to look out for me as a way to protect me. My neighbor was a gate keeper.

There was a time when one of my other neighbors asked me to babysit her daughter. I was excited because it was my first paying job. She later shared with me, "I noticed that you were home alone and I thought it be better if you two were together." This neighbor was a gatekeeper too, and her insight was spot on. I needed her daughter as much as her little girl needed me. We laughed together and made great memories over the years.

As she became curious about boys, I gave her sound advice about how to remain focused while having fun. I became a gatekeeper for her. I will always remember the day she was invited to attend a school dance by her crush. She was excited and her convictions were strong at an early age. The young lady told me, "I was clear with him, his hands do not belong on my body." They had a great time at the dance.

Another couple hired me to be their babysitter for occasional date nights. They'd encountered me yet I never noticed them. In their observations I was "poised and independent." They often saw me and another black girl walking the mile from school to the public bus stop. They asked the school secretary about me and decided I would be a great fit for their daughters. I was anxious when they asked for my number to call my mom and ask her permission.

She gave her consent for me to babysit, and Mr. Long picked me up to watch his two lil' brown girls. I had no idea how to get to their home because it was not on the bus line. It was in a beautiful area with single-family homes. The streets were lined with trees and each home had its own driveway. When we got to his house, his wife would give me instructions for the evening. She'd say, "The girls have already eaten, and they are ready for bed."

By the time I read them a story or put on a movie, they would be nodding off. When the girls would see me at school, they would wave joyfully and I would give them quick a high five or a hug before I said, "Get back in line with your class." Mr. Long and his wife paid me well to care for them in their absence.

The following year he hired me to be an administrative assistant at the company he owned. It was my first corporate job. He taught me everything I needed to know to be successful and kept me accountable for my mistakes, too.

One afternoon he thanked me for modeling for his daughters what it was like to be a Black girl at a predominately White school. "I observed that you did not assimilate or transform to be accepted. You are your true self."

Mr. Long explained that it was important to him and his wife for their girls to have someone to look up to. I lost touch with the family once I went to college, but I am sure the girls grew up to be amazing women. He was a gatekeeper, yet a fierce protector and advocate for them. Recently my dad ran into them in the market and he told me they are doing well. Unfortunately, he didn't get their contact information. I hope to reconnect with them on social media one day.

My gift of discernment started in my early childhood and it has served me well throughout my life. I can relate to people, and I have the ability to hear the things that they are not saying out loud. I can hear cries behind a person's dry eyes, and I can see them holding their breath hoping no one can sense their insecurities. I treasure my gift of being a gatekeeper and a role model.

I am Unshakeable

I am loved, and always have been.
I just couldn't see it past the walls.

In me is power presence and purpose

I'm resilient relentless and respected
I'm passionate complex and impactful

I am light and life
I am healing

I am Latifa and my peace is unshakable

I fought for her
I'm set apart
I'm grateful that
Ruth,
Lena,
Ella and Naomi
blazed the trail for me.

I am because of them.
Because of them I am.

Because of them I can grab my sisters
Who are hiding pain in their eyes.

I can pour into them.
I am designed to be my sisters keeper.

PRAYER OF AFFIRMATION

Lord,

Help me to trust the unique way You formed my voice, my perspective, and my thoughts. I release thoughts of inferiority and embrace the way You have designed me.

When I look in the mirror I see my full lips, long legs, and my perfect brown skin. My eyes are beautiful, and so are the kinks in my hair. I see how my nostrils lift when I breathe, and I appreciate everything I view in the mirror. The woman looking back at me matters.

I am amazing, brave, and bold. My smile is inviting. There is power in me. I hear myself even when I feel voiceless. Sometimes my words trigger others when they touch places people thought were hidden. Even when they don't want to hear my truth, I will keep speaking. I won't stop sharing my truth.

Taking care of myself is worth it.

Amen.

Unshakeable

STORM CLOUDS PRODUCE PURPOSE

*Please be advised that this chapter contains situations of sexual violence. Although it was hard to write, it was necessary.

In April of 2022, I attended a self-care retreat. My hope was to be a silent participant; I was looking forward to having the speakers pour into me spiritually. Instead, I was shaken up like a good martini when the topics of rape and abortion were raised during the conversation.

I wanted to join the conversation, but I hesitated. I thought to myself, "How do I tell them that I had an abortion, yet I was a virgin?" The hardest part wasn't talking about the abortion. I asked myself, "How do I explain that I actually had more than one abortion?" Sitting there, my mind was racing. "How do I explain that the first time something foreign entered my body was when the nurse inserted the speculum inside of me at the clinic?"

I didn't talk about that experience for a long time because it was hard to explain. People wouldn't have understood or even believed my situation if I told them. Throughout the years I did not want to talk about it, because the thought made me feel like the young 13-year-old girl that I was at the time. When the subject was brought up at the retreat, there I was, feeling stuck.

I knew that because of my first experience with sex, many parts of me stopped growing. I was already going through a lot being a brown girl trying to fit in a White world. At the White school, I was too black. In my Black neighborhood, I was too White. Unable to find my place, I found solace with boys who enjoyed talking to me. The boys around me always understood me. They were intrigued by what I had to say, and they listened to me. My male friends were engaged and seemed vested in me. I felt safe and heard.

The girls around me were acting self-absorbed and they did not want to listen to me. With them, everything was competitive and petty. Adults didn't wanna listen either and they devalued most of what I had to share. I felt misunderstood by most people and just went with the flow seeking a space where I could go to be celebrated and appreciated.

Oddly enough, I managed to be an example for younger girls around me. The younger girls depended on me to help them work through their situations and I became a place of solace for many of them. They listened to me and sought my advice, which validated my wisdom. I don't know how it turned out that way, but it did.

In a limited way, I learned to use my voice to advocate for others and bring them a sense of peace. But when it came to me being a pregnant virgin, I didn't know how to give it words. I was embarrassed and ashamed and at times, still am.

Having an abortion changed me. I still remember what I wore that day. Purple jeans. When I close my eyes, I can still see the examination room and how I felt when I walked into that cold space. I felt alone and unsupported sitting in that room. I did not know what to expect, or the gravity of the situation.

When the nurse picked up the speculum, I asked her, "What is that thing? I have never seen anything like it before." Instead of telling me it was a speculum and explaining the purpose of the tool, she responded in a condescending tone, "It's no bigger than what got you here." This was a defining moment for all of the wrong reasons. When the nurse spoke to me that way, I wanted to question her, but instead, I sat in silence and went numb while she did her job.

Internally I was screaming. I wanted to tell them what happened to me and force them to explain what they were about to do to me. Sitting in that examination room with my mom, I was deflated and defeated, which led to me losing my voice and my power.

Years after that experience, I terminated other pregnancies because I thought I needed to be perfect before I would be worthy of having a child. I chose not to give birth because I had not become the woman that I once needed in my life. I have been blessed to be the parent of a bonus daughter and a biological son, both successful well-adjusted young adults. Ironically, when I recognize gaps in my parenting, I still wonder if it is rooted in those early decisions to terminate pregnancies as if I am being punished for my choices.

When I lost my voice and my power, I just wanted peace and I needed to feel heard. Somehow, I knew that I needed to create safe spaces for girls who don't have the necessities that they needed from adults.

Shaken Like a Martini

Over the years, I have had many experiences that caused me to question my worth. One of them was being sexually violated by someone I happily dated for years.

50

He was not an aggressive man, nor did he meet the stereotype of a "rapist." We were friends and lovers who shared great college memories together. We clicked instantly and soon after our first meeting we hung out laughing for hours, eating, and enjoying each other's company.

He was kind, confident and funny. This man was easy on the eyes and intelligent. I was drawn to his determination, drive and energy. Our relationship carried me after coming off what had been an amazing relationship that began to rapidly dissolve.

It was a consensual encounter until it wasn't. It quickly turned into a violation when he took what he wanted for his pleasure without my permission. "Wait. Ouch. Move. STOP!" He stopped only after he was finished. Maybe saying "No" would have changed things. Maybe instead of squirming and trying to get away, he would have understood that my screams were not from pleasure.

I could see remorse in his eyes. He said, "Sorry. I didn't mean to hurt you." He held me as hot tears fell from my eyes. I didn't have the strength to gather my things and leave. I lay there for what felt like hours until I gathered my strength to get up. Eventually, I walked home, alone. The incident crushed me and left me physically in pain and emotionally depleted.

Things were never the same in our relationship after that day. The guy couldn't even look at me with a straight face when I accidentally ran into him. I tried to avoid places if I thought we'd cross paths. I questioned if what we had was even a real relationship. "Perhaps I was just a good time," I thought to myself.

Our involvement ended and I felt a loneliness inside of me that I could not describe. I was reshaped by that damaging experience.

Running To God

To get some solitude, I spent a lot of time alone in a park that I loved. I watched the trees move freely in the wind and the birds soar in the blue sky. At the park, the clouds changed shape with ease and painted God's artwork across the sky. Flowers bloomed and the sun was warm on my skin. I was grounded and safe in the park.

I moved on from the experience of being sodomized. I was seeking something to restore me, but I didn't know what I was looking for. I turned back to God, and He embraced me. My salvation is what kept me then, and what keeps me now. God is my peace and my refuge. He has never forsaken me. Only God knew what I had been through because I had not told anyone what happened until I wrote this book. Thank you, Abba, Father.

Because I was seeking God, I started to reflect on my grandmother and her prayers for me. I remembered the songs she taught me like "This Little Light of Mine I'm gonna let it shine." In my 20's it felt like those memories were all I had to hold on to. I wondered what happened to little Latifa. I wondered, "How did she lose her innocence?" I felt like she gave it away in search of comfort, safety, and acceptance. The little girl in me did not know she was worth fighting for.

I stuffed my feelings away until they couldn't fit inside of me anymore. The secrets I carried were heavy, but I was convinced if I hid them, they wouldn't be seen. My secrets stained my soul and holding them was hurting me. I put up a wall to hide the pain and shame. My pain caused me to question my worth.

My college roommate was my friend from high school. She was funny, adventurous, full of life and God-fearing. My friend modeled her faith to me. I saw her prayer closet and watched how she trusted God. On a day that I found myself broken and overflowing with pain, I ran to my room and cried out to God.

I knew that He was real because my grandmother and best friend knew Him well and I had seen Him move in their lives. I hoped that God would recognize me and meet me in my secret place. I fell to the floor and cried. I told Him everything: all my insecurities, all my secrets, all my shame. I had a lot of work to do to tear down the walls between us.

I was vulnerable with Him. I exposed my heart and let go of my secrets. My purpose was hindered by my secrets. Holding them kept me captive to the bondage. I needed to breathe and acknowledge my pain. I needed to tell my story and process the journey I'd been on and find my power. I told God, "I feel worthless, and this is all my fault." I shared my truth, with all my heart to God. He heard my cries and I felt comforted even though I was alone.

My roommate was at work when this happened, but her boyfriend was a contractor, so I called him hoping he'd be free to take my call. He knew God too. I was still weeping and sniffling when he picked up and I began sharing with him what I experienced. "I don't know what this means or how it will change my life. "

He explained, "This is salvation." He told me, "You have given your heart to God."

When I accepted Christ, I was forever changed. I found a sense of belonging in my surrender to God. As I reflect on that day, I realize that I was transformed in my time alone with God, my Abba, Father.

I am my best when I am alone with God. He has always been there to cover me. He saw me just as I was and accepted me. He became my helper and my sounding board. God constantly reminds me that I am called and that I am fearfully and wonderfully made.

So many things happened in my life that tried to silence me. I did not understand why I had to endure so many storms, but I shared my story and experience at the self-care retreat. My voice is a gift, and it is time to tell my story. I was fully healed from my shame. There is no longer an invisible cloud hovering over me. I can say with confidence that I am enough, I always have been, and I always will be. Every storm eventually will run out of rain.

"Every storm eventually will run out of rain."

~Latifa Miller

ADVOCATING FOR OTHERS

Several years ago, I attended a workshop and all of the participants were asked to bring a childhood photo. The facilitator led an exercise where we as participants, were asked to share with the group the dreams of the little girl in the picture. I had no clue what to say, because lil' Latifa was just existing at that age.

I don't remember her dreams or aspirations. I don't remember having a favorite color, a favorite food, or a favorite movie. I don't know if I stuffed these memories away, or if they never existed.

During my high school years, I noticed a pattern within me of being uncomfortable with unrest. I didn't do well with injustice. Unbeknownst to me, I was becoming an advocate for underrepresented people. I developed a desire to be a better person for the young girls who would follow in my footsteps. In my high school years, I helped develop Cultural Awareness for Everyone, a minority Awareness group. We called it C.A.F.É. The acronym was a softer way of saying "Ya'll just don't get us, but you're gonna learn!"

In college, I served in a leadership role in the Black Action Society and was always involved in addressing policy and creating space for our voices to be heard and understood. I interned at the local public Broadcasting station for a program called Black Horizons - the nation's longest-running public affairs program for an African-American audience.

My first job out of college was in social services. The theme of advocacy followed me and has made a way for me to use my voice in a meaningful way for the disenfranchised, underserved and overlooked.

Daughters of Zion

Decades after college, I started a non-profit, Daughters of Zion, which is designed to create a space for unseen girls. I remembered myself as a pre-teen who gravitated toward whoever showed me attention. I was seeking to be heard, noticed, and validated so I created the safe place for good girls and unseen women that I needed.

"Bad girls" receive attention for their exposed mistakes, but there are not enough programs designed for good girls who make mistakes, but succeed without getting caught by their mess because people don't see it.

In my work, I intentionally serve "good girls" because their needs are often overlooked. Daughters of Zion helps these girls transition through adolescence without judgment. We build trusting relationships and help them navigate through their experiences, so they don't have to turn to strangers when things get rough.

My broken pieces and ugly truths gave me purpose. When I look in the eyes of the young girls I work with, I reach beyond the walls and let them know that I see them and the shame they try to hide. I tell them, "I remember what it is like having to hold your breath waiting for a safe space to exhale. I know what it is like to have to keep going when your peace is lacking." I am honest and transparent and seek to build trust and accountability between us because I understand my role as a gatekeeper.

Impactful

Be intentional about being impactful,
tomorrow is not promised.

Today has great value and is in front of you.

Take every opportunity to make sure that you
are being impactful

An impact on the people whose lives you
encounter,

An impact on the meaningful work you do

Be mindful

You are leaving a footprint

Your legacy is being created and
Your future is being determined

Make an impact today

"I am qualified. I am capable.
I am not a failure. I am not less than.
I am good enough. I've got this."

~Latifa Miller

Stay True To Yourself

Stay true to yourself
Dig deep and figure out exactly who you are
called to be

Walk in your purpose

Be your authentic self

Understand what brings you joy and what it
takes to keep your peace

The best way to be your best self is to be your
true self

Learn to love your flaws,
they make you unique
and set you apart.

Stay true to your calling

Latifa Miller

*"Positivity is a choice.
I will not focus on the
negativity."*

~Latifa Miller

EMBRACING ME

After my sexual trauma, I began exploring life on my terms and it was eye-opening for me. I was beginning to have amazing encounters with God and I enjoyed them. Up until that point I usually stood out when I was in groups of people, but during that time I was embracing my unique abilities. Accepting the fact that God has set me apart from others allowed me to discover my purpose, embrace my calling, and understand my anointing.

I had prayer partners who prayed with me and held me accountable. I was able to create spaces to explore what energized me. This was the season in my life when my love for worshiping God was developed. In my quiet, still time, I began to learn more about the importance of being my authentic self and using the power of my voice. The words I spoke made a difference and they empowered others. When life had been complex and stormy, I never realized the importance of the authority God had given to me.

As I rested in God and grew my faith, I began to understand His grace over my life. I had experienced what it was like to be misunderstood and overlooked. Often, I felt compelled to speak life into people who were not so sure of themselves. I was giving to people what I needed.

In those reflection times, I realized that the areas of my life that had been attacked, torn down, and silenced in my adolescence were my strengths. These revelations took me on a spiritually awakening soul search. I reflected on what I valued in my life and the genuine relationships that were beneficial to me. Sisterhood and meaningful connections were at the top of the list of what matters to me.

In my adulthood I participated in a professional leadership program; my group was challenged to discover our innate skills and talents by reconnecting with someone from our childhood. My friend Skylar who had lived across the street was a consistent friend for me growing up. I asked, and she agreed to help me. Growing up all the boys had their eye on her because she was pretty and confident. I asked her to describe me for the assignment and she used descriptive words such as focused, different with individuality, challenged yet excelled, self-sufficient, selfless, independent, respectful, excellent, and communicator. The words that made me cry, "You made others feel important, even when you barely knew them."

I asked myself, "We were children, how could she have known these things? How could I have been all these things when I felt alone and unseen?" My spiritual journey revealed to me that my perception and lack of self-worth stemmed from trauma, not truth. While I couldn't see what she and others saw in me, it was still my truth and part of my story. My friend was a gatekeeper.

Around this same time, another friend, Marie, reminded me of a letter I mailed to her while I was in college. She was in high school struggling to navigate her life, and our bond was secure, so secure that I will take her secrets to the grave with me. I often encouraged her by telling her that her life mattered. I would say, "Validation from a relationship will not fill your brokenness."

In my letter, I reminded her that what she was chasing would not resolve her pain and I told her about the peace I had found in God. Talking to Marie about that letter, I thought about the phone call she made when she got my letter. We talked, cried, and dug into complicated matters until she felt lighter. I was relieved when I heard the smile in her voice before we hung up. Our relationship continues this way. I was there as she navigated the impact of loss associated with COVID-19, and the dynamics my Goddaughters, her beautiful angels, are facing in their adult lives. Marie too was a gatekeeper.

As I was navigating what I believed was abandonment and being unlovable, God was revealing His truth to me through these individuals. Along the journey I met a beautiful soul, Nia, who gifted me a framed scripture from Jeremiah 29:11. It is a very common scripture that many know, yet it is personal for me. As my life was shifting to understand my purpose, this message of hope and its promise carried me:

"For I know the plans I have for you, declares the Lord, plans for welfare and not for evil, to give you a future and a hope."

Over and over, I have been affirmed and rebuilt into the woman God has called me to be. I am grounded in my womanhood despite the negative circumstances I faced growing up that could have shaped me differently. My husband has also contributed greatly to who I am.

The first words that my husband said when we first met on our college campus were, "Hello Sunshine."

These words confirmed that I was walking with God. I was glowing because my faith was strong. Those words were also a prophetic indication of my calling to be an example of God's light and love. Matthew 5:16 says, "In the same way, let your light shine before others, that they may see your good deeds and glorify your Father in heaven." In that season, I was living alone for the first time, learning new things about myself. I was finding my footing and coming into my womanhood.

My husband and I were friends throughout college. We had lots of fun, created great memories, and had many late night conversations after campus union parties. We never dated each other, but our connection was strong.

After I graduated, we didn't see each other often, yet we reconnected at a time in my life when I was unwavering in my walk with God. Since the day we met, my husband has brought out the best in me and allowed me to shine as my authentic self. I am the sunshine that he saw that day and we walk together leading people to Christ.

I am grateful that he allows me to shine, and that God had allowed me to embrace His love and strengthen my self-love before we met. Together my husband and I are a force to be reckoned with.

Part III - Find Your Unshakeable Peace

Unshakeable

HEALING WORK

In order to achieve unshakeable peace, healing work is a required part of your journey. I do not recommend that you stuff your pain inside. You can let it out by screaming, yelling, or crying— just get it out. There is power in releasing your hurt, pain, and shame. Letting it out will free you to press through your challenging circumstances and it will motivate you to find the things that drive your purpose.

There may be a lot of distractions going on in the world and there is certainly a lot of noise, yet I want you to choose to focus on what brings you joy. Believe in your dreams and never lose hope. Believe that everything will work out in your favor. When you are in a space of unrest be intentional about finding your peace and joy. Any crisis in your life will challenge you to stand in your truth.

In order to have the kind of faith, joy, and peace that is unshakable, stay consistent and don't allow distractions to take you off your mark. Do not sit on your calling. It is time to get up from your place of shame and pursue the call on your life.

Unshakeable PEACE

"I will not be closed to possibility.
I will not be limited.
I will open myself and spread out.

~Latifa Miller

Here are some steps I want to offer to help you break out of shame, find your purpose, and maintain your unshakeable peace:

Fight for Your Authentic Self

Fight to find space for yourself. Fight to understand what your authentic self looks like. Fight to not allow someone else to define it for you. Fight to have peace of mind and not to feel like you must be like the fabled Superwoman. Take your cape off and take time to cry if you need to, or just sit silently.

If the people around you are judging you, you have the wrong people in your front row. You probably need a shift in your life if the people around you are distracting or are creating noise and chatter that takes away from your peace. It is okay to break away. It might feel weird, but that freedom is necessary.

Authenticity is about your presence, living in the moment with conviction and confidence, and staying true to yourself. Why are you seeking perfection instead of authenticity? Perfection is unattainable and not sustainable. It's a trap and a delusion. You are not limited to what happened in your past. Cherish the moments of each day and remember what happens is a part of your purpose journey.

I encourage you to enjoy life on your own terms. Don't allow your circumstances to discourage or allow you to become grumpy or bitter. Sometimes you will be tested. Shame can't restrict you if you remain in character and maintain your control. Maintaining peace on the path is as important as the destination.

You can uphold your boundaries because you have everything that you need and most of what you want. You are blessed, and as you shine, you bless others.

Embrace Change

Too many of us are still trying to hold on to life as it was. Be willing to do a NEW THING! You can feel it when things are changing. It is exciting, but you feel so uncertain all at the same time. This is exactly how change hits us.

If you're not careful, you'll stay in a place of indecisiveness for far too long. A wise woman once told me to trust my gut. And she would often say, "Your knower knows." That stuck with me because your "knower" does know. You can call it your "gut reaction", your "intuition," or your "discernment," the fact is that something inside of you is guiding you. That little voice inside of you is there to teach you and to help you navigate. You must be intentional about listening to it. The best way to listen to God is sit quietly so you know the difference between the still, small voice and the noise, or clutter of the world.

When your "knower" is talking to you, nothing around you stops. The chaos is still happening, the buzz is happening, the busyness and the agenda items are all still happening, but your "knower" taps you on the shoulder. "Hey," it says. "Hey, hey sis, you might want to consider this." It might say, "Hey, you should slow down. Watch out. Be careful." Or "Don't do that. Go left. Go right. Don't go at all."

I have found comfort and peace in my still, small voice. Sometimes I listened to it, and other times I didn't. Every time, it let me know that I could trust myself. It is very important for you to build this muscle. As you do this, you can teach others how to listen to and understand the language of their own still, small voice. You may hear your still, small voice and make a different choice, but give yourself grace along the way.

Grace is the thing that allows you to continue to soar because it shows you new opportunities. Grace is the thing that allows you to continue to be free because you know that you are forgiven for your sins. Grace allows you to remain courageous because each day you start with brand new mercies.

Grace won't let you stop because as you keep moving and shaking, you keep trying. Grace prevents you from doubting yourself and living in regret. Grace can be your peace of mind because you look for opportunities to apologize when you are wrong. Grace is your do over like Maya Angelou said, "When you know better, you do better." These may sound like clichés but allow these gems to strengthen you as you stand in your truth.

Remember, your "knower" knows. Trust the journey and keep it moving, sis. You must give your all in this life in order to get everything out of it that you are supposed to. Don't leave anything on the table. Live your best life because you deserve it. I am no longer frozen in grief because I am confident in who I am, and that makes me free to be myself. I want that for you too.

Find something to be thankful for, something to dance and to have joy about. Discover something to put a smile on your face, no matter what your circumstances are.

Ask for Help

I am blessed and highly favored by people in my circle who are supportive and encouraging. Sometimes I have needed to throw in the towel and say, "Hey, I'm not okay and I need my sisters and my aunties to help."

Having people who won't judge you or remind you of your shortcomings is helpful. That is what sisters do. Whether it is your sorority, church family, sister friends, or family you need someone you can call on. Surround yourself with people who inspire and motivate you.

Find Balance

I've learned that balance comes when you have both peace and purpose because they go hand-in-hand. When you understand what you are called to do it brings peace. When you have peace, you value your purpose. One, without the other, is discord. When you aren't balanced you spend too much time trying to find peace, clarity and understanding. You get lost looking, yet everything you need is within you. When you don't have balance, you disqualify yourself and can become defeated.

You must figure out what balance is for you and try not to model what you see someone else doing. Balance doesn't have to look like two kids and a white picket fence. Discipline will keep you focused.

Balance is about having peace of mind. Balance is about moving in a way that is not haphazard; it is intentional. It is not just about checking everything off of your to-do list, it really is about having a sense of purpose and understanding that the things that you do or don't do are all about the things you are called to do. It takes a presence that requires a lot of energy. You have to be focused and mindful. You cannot willy-nilly your way to balance because you won't be walking in purpose or be your authentic self. Balance has a lot to do with being authentic.

I am learning a lot about my calling. I am an empty nester and that brings a different focus. What I recognize is that I am truly called to give wisdom to women. In order to give someone, the wisdom that is for them I have to be able to be still and be quiet to hear and discern when I am supposed to speak. The anointing isn't always scripted, you have to be obedient to it. My opinions may be unpopular, yet they are necessary for that one girl or perhaps woman sitting in the room hoping to be seen and understood.

Prioritize your life. You might need to take a trip to see your favorite aunt. Sit at her feet and let her pour into you. You are never too busy for balance.

Balance can be getting a meal preparation service, so you don't have to cook every day. One time my husband came into the kitchen and asked, "Why are you doing that?" I was trying to cook dinner. I tried to give an explanation and he said, "Nobody asked you to do that, and it is depleting you. Your disposition is going to be off. We don't want that negative effect. If we need to eat pizza so you can keep your peace of mind, okay, we will eat pizza. It is going to be okay."

I was a young mom trying to check off boxes about what a "good mom and wife" is supposed to do, but those things were not necessarily what my family needed.

Do Not Compare Yourself to Others

Don't compare yourself to other people. If they are doing fantastic cheer them on but understand there is room for everybody. God made us with a specific purpose and there is space for your purpose. Someone else's purpose won't take up or intrude on the space that God has designed for you. Don't allow those fears to play games in your mind. The enemy has a strategy to destroy you, tear you down, and prevent you from walking in your purpose.

The enemy is cool with you doing great things as long as you are not doing what God has called you to do. As long as you are off schedule and out of sync the enemy is cool

because you are not doing what you are
supposed to do.

Balance is important and it requires giving
yourself grace. Balance requires forgiving
yourself and looking forward to the future.
Someone will always tell you that you are off.
Will you listen to them?

Be Grateful

Start your day off full of joy and full of
grace and thankful for God's mercy. Look for
simple things like waking up in the sunshine,
having peace of mind, having good
health, having family members and a support
system. Think about how your strength and
resilience play into your peace of mind and
your ability to be successful. As seasons
change, see how much there is to be grateful
for by latching on to God's peace and finding
a way to rest in His goodness.

I am the light. I show up and I am
intentional to bring my light energy.
I've been through something but when I
reflect, I understand that my joy, compassion,
and energy make a difference. When you
allow your light to shine, it can't help but
extend itself outside of YOU to others around
you!

We all carry heaviness. Until you figure
out the best way to lighten your load, don't

just fake it till you make it. I encourage you to recognize how much energy it takes to pretend that you're something that you're not. Take that same energy to build yourself into what you need to be. Equip yourself to walk authentically in the areas that you are called to walk.

Get Quiet

Sometimes I need reminders that all is well in the world. There is so much noise and it is critical for me to get still in the presence of God. This quiet time allows me to get clarity. I have to get clarity from God to learn how to change lives. When I need clarity, I go to the park and sit near a waterfall. Listening to the water and birds singing relaxes me. Sometimes I look for smiling babies or children playing in the park which makes me laugh, too.

When I am with God, I am reminded of the power of peace.

If I have a lot of noise in my life, then I might not hear God. By not hearing God, I miss opportunities or say the wrong thing at the wrong time with the wrong tone and the wrong tempo. Tone matters when God has given you something to deposit into someone's life. When you are depositing God's seed, the timing has to be right.

I don't thrive in crazy. I can see how that has been a thread throughout my life. I find myself being the peacemaker or the level-setter when there is chaos around me. When things were unjust, it never sat well with me. If you feel out of balance, perhaps you are not sitting still long enough to quiet your mind.

I learned some of my hardest lessons about balance from my son. When he was growing up, I could sense when he needed space. We had a code word when he needed a break. In his youth, he would say to me, "Mom, I think you're just tired. I think you are doing too much." He was exactly right.

Your body talks to you, learn to listen to it. We are on a big kick about self-care. Many people define it as getting your hair done and getting your nails done, but it is a little different to me. Self-care is about knowing who you are and understanding that. When you know yourself, you can listen to your body.

When I am overly emotional, and my response doesn't match the situation, I know I am out of balance. Think about it, if you are on your way to church trying to run somebody over, that road rage is an indicator that you are unbalanced. If you are jealous or envious of someone instead of allowing yourself to admire them, you are unbalanced. When your responses tend to lean to the ncgative space instead of the positive space sometimes that means something is off within you.

Stand on the Shoulders of Giants

So much trauma has stolen the soul of our ancestors and that trauma followed me, and my peace was constantly snatched away. Like my ancestors, I have kept showing up in life and giving my all. Just as they kept fighting to overcome, so did I.

We all stand on someone else's shoulders. If you read Genesis, Eve, the first woman, paved the way for all of us. She was created by God with intentionality. She stood in the face of adversity. She won, she lost, and she won again. Eve birthed life. She was loved and adored by Adam.

We stand on the shoulders of our ancestors. They created opportunities and we are able to share our gifts and vision with others. We are fertile ground and abundance comes from us because of them. We have a purpose, and we must produce fruit. Our ancestors support our shine.

Hannah in the bible was ridiculed and continued to show up. Maya Angelou wrote an example of her in her poem "Still I Rise"

Like dust, I rise.
I rise.
I rise.

Hannah bore good fruit and because of her faith, we are here. Hannah was a woman of her word who lived in gratitude.

In Samuel chapter 1 of the Bible, Hannah was overlooked and dismissed, yet full of purpose. As a wife, at times Hannah felt hopeless and rejected because her husband had other wives who had children. Through the taunts and jeers of the other women, Hannah held on to the promise of God and it eventually manifested in her life.

Hannah kept pressing and believing that her desires would be fulfilled. As the story unfolded, it was Hannah who became the answer that was needed when God's anointing came through her. I can relate to Hannah because she was the curse breaker. So am I. I stand on the shoulders of Ruth, Naomi & Lena.

Never forget that you are the breakthrough for other Black Women to find their strength. Stand tall in your unshakeable peace.

Unshakeable
PEACE

*"I learn from life and
I am stronger because of
what I have experienced."*

~Latifa Miller

Real Talk

I don't like holidays

My heart is full, yet I struggle to breathe

Everyone flicks to their tribes and enjoys
their traditions,
but my memories are gone,
and I never regained my footing.

The new tradition is uncertainty and low-
key anxiety.

I become uncertain of things I thought I
knew, and the cycle is frustrating.

Perhaps being enough isn't something I'll
know and feeling inadequate in my own
life is the norm.

I'm unsure if others see my unreadiness in
my eyes, but they don't say much.

As soon as I think I've figured it out,
things fall apart.
It's the holidays.
I work on being approachable
but they still walk away....

As I left my child last Thanksgiving
morning I felt empty.

As I headed home I felt empty.
As I did my work I felt empty.
The exhaustion is real.

I need the Lord to fill me because my
friends think I'm okay
or busy and don't even bother
to check-in, they will leave me bc.

Selah

In that moment I learned that the roles I
play are just that, roles.
They are what I do, not who I am.

Learning what really fills and
understanding my purpose
is my life's mission.

Knowing my worth and power gives me
breath.

This holiday season I hope I'll find my
footing.

"I am equipped to succeed."

~Latifa Miller

Questions for Reflection

Unshakeable
PEACE

+ Who do you share your hopes and dreams with?

+ When you talk about your hopes and dreams do you become accountable to them?

+ Do you feel worthy of your desires?

+ Do you know that you are capable of achieving your dreams and that you deserve to walk in your purpose and calling?

+ What can you do to bring your dreams to life?

+ What memories do you have of your dad?

+ What have you wanted to ask your parents but never had the opportunity?

+ If you have ever been the only Black woman/girl in an all-White environment, what did you learn about yourself during that time?

+ Do you understand your purpose?

+ Do you know that you are victorious in the things that you were called to do by God? This knowledge will motivate you when you get off track.

+ Do you allow your big dreams to make you feel like something is wrong with you?

+ Why do you think "bad" girls are given a lot of attention, and "good" girls who do "bad things" are not?

+ What was your experience as a "good girl doing bad things" or a girl labeled as "bad" because you did bad things?

+ Have you thought about why you do the things you do for others?

+ Do you shrink back from using your voice or do you speak up?

Part IV – Affirmations

Unshakeable

On the following pages are a list of
affirmations that I believe will help you get to
your unshakeable peace.

I recommend that you speak the words out
loud at least once a day to strengthen your
self-confidence. Write the affirmations in your
journal. The more you use them, the more
you will believe what you speak. As you affirm
yourself in God, you will break out of shame,
discover your worth and find your peace.

Confidence + Self-Love Affirmations

I matter and I belong. Period.

I can do it just as I am.

I listen closely to my "knower," it always knows. I trust my gut because it will not fail me.

I am walking through my fears and tears.

I am already great!

I will be the best version of me.

I can control my own happiness.

I am EQUIPPED!

I remembered who I am, and the game changed!!!!

I do not worry about how the story ends because in the end I win!

I have access to the resources I need to thrive.

I am authentically me and I am enough.

I am resilient.

I prioritize ME.

I belong.

I am strong, smart, pretty, and worthy enough.

No one can compare me to another. I am Uniquely ME.

I deserve the best.

I am capable, qualified, valuable, deserving, and WORTH IT!

I am focused and intentional.

The best person to be is Me!
I inspire others.

I am not forgotten; in fact, I am unforgettable.

I deserve love.

I make the world better by being my authentic self.

I am capable & unstoppable.

I am beautiful.

I choose to be motivated, not manipulated.

I choose to be useful, not used.
I choose me!

I will always be kind to myself.

I will always value and appreciate myself.

I will always be myself.

Every part of me is worthy, specifically, the parts that hurt.
I give thanks.

I am wonderful. I matter. I deserve peace, joy, love, and compassion.

I will learn to be intentional about how I spend my priceless time.

To love myself I must like her. To like her I must respect her. To respect her I must accept her. To accept her I must know her. I will get to know her, all of her. She needs me!

I am limitless, and I have what it takes. I have the strength to finish.

I am Powerful. I am Brilliant. I am Special. I am Unique. I am Strong. I am loved. I am Kind

I am WHOLE, I am BRAVE, and I believe in ME!

My smile brings me joy. It breaks down walls and reminds me I am okay just as I am.

My words matter. My actions matter. I will be intentional about the energy I bring along with me. I will behave accordingly, not haphazardly.

I won't shrink. I will fully and unapologetically be me.

It's my time. It's time for a new story, a new direction, and new dreams.

My vulnerability is my strength.

It's okay if I can't handle everything today.

I am loved, chosen, and accepted as I am.

I am confident, capable, and loved.

I dream big and will achieve my dreams.

When I look in the mirror, I know I am cared for, and I was created to walk in my purpose.

I will listen to my inner voice; it will not mislead me. I will get to know my hopes and dreams so the noise of the world will not distract me.

I am beautiful, I believe in MYSELF! Others do too.

I will think big. I will dream big. I will believe in the impossible because success is achievable and mine for the taking.

I will survive.

I am Amazing. I try my best.

I deserve love, peace, and compassion.

I deserve to be noticed. I deserve to get better. I do not have all of the answers.

I control my thoughts and actions.

I am the energy I desire to attract.
I will enjoy my journey.

I am disciplined, consistent, and patient.

I am magnetic, free, and powerful.

I am creative, transcendent, and the best part of HER!

I am unstoppable.

I believe in myself.

I live my truth.

I will get up.

I ask for help, then accept it.
I look for the solutions.

I focus on my strengths.

I am one of one and I choose myself every time.

I am fruitful with my gifts.

Healing + Gratitude Affirmations

When I forgive, I heal. When I let go, I grow.

I always speak good things to myself.

I am blessed. I am free and I am forgiven.

I matter and I am seen.

I am AUTHENTICALLY Me!

When I see my sister I do not judge her. If I see something that bothers me, I let her off the hook so I can get free, too.

I do not recycle negativity.

I make the best of good and bad days. It's not about perfection, it's about the progress gained on the journey. No one has it all together. My struggle is part of the journey.

Confusion works itself out.

I elevate my perspective and evolve into the woman I was meant to be.

My broken pieces and ugly truths, they make me a beautiful masterpiece with purpose.

I do not doubt myself. I have what it takes to succeed.

I don't hate the circumstances that make me who I am.

I embrace my pain and it will lead me to my passion.

I elevate, explore, and embrace me!

Complexities build me. I embrace the hard parts and learn to move through them. I accept the process and allow it to build me.

I have compassion for the parts of me that doubted me.

My challenges teach me.

I am thankful for where I am and excited for where I am going.

I'm unstoppable and full of gratitude.

I celebrate myself and those I love.

I am healing. I have grace and compassion.

I am grateful, compassionate, and energetic.

I give people their flowers now.

I forgive myself for underestimating my worth.

I am learning to just "be."

Love + Faith Affirmations

I will live loved. I will live fearlessly. I will live unrestricted.

I will be loving, kind and peaceful so I can experience love, kindness, and peace.

I will encourage others.

I am strong. When I feel weak I will not fall apart. I will use my power to rebuild my strength.

I support my sister; she needs me, and I need her.

I choose faith over fear. Both require me to believe in something that I can't see.

I am prepared and equipped to face any challenge with peace and calm.

Self-Care + Peace Affirmations

I rest as needed.

I don't give up.

I take time to water my soul and feed my spirit so I can blossom.

I watch the words I speak to myself. She's listening and she hears me. I will be kind to myself because I deserve to be loved, heard, seen, and understood.

I have peace and joy.

I will find my tribe, I need them.

I am willing to embrace the journey.

I will take my power back.

I will embrace my sensitivity.
I will be flexible today because I will need the same grace tomorrow.

I am careful not to play a superhero role. I will not allow my invisible cape to choke the life out of me.

"I am Latifa and I Am Enough!"

~Latifa Miller

ABOUT THE AUTHOR

 Latifa Miller is a devoted mother and loving wife who lives in Pittsburgh, Pennsylvania. Growing up in Philadelphia, Pennsylvania she adopted fierce grit, strong determination, and faith from many loved ones in her community.

A graduate of the University of Pittsburgh, Latifa vowed at a young age to share her testimony with young women, giving them a road map to navigate growing into womanhood and finding success. She believes that sharing your testimony not only has the power to heal, guide, and teach others, it prevents you from hiding behind your own secrets and shame.

After witnessing young girls seek attention in the wrong places to validate their worth, Latifa founded Daughters of Zion 101 (DOZ) in 2011. DOZ's mission is to create a safe place for young girls to grow into adulthood and learn without judgment. More information can be found on their website: (https://www.daughtersofzion101.org/)

Latifa serves her community through membership in many organizations and several board appointments including Zeta Phi Beta Sorority, Incorporated.

ACKNOWLEDGMENTS

To my amazing Family **Kevin, Kiana, and Naim** thank you for loving me.

Thank you to my **Unpluckable Squad** who encouraged me through the writing of this book.

La Dina, Maisha, Nakea and **Charmaine**, thank you for your support that carried me to the finish line.

Special thanks to my Scribe Coach, **Penda L. James** who believed in me throughout this project.

Made in the USA
Middletown, DE
31 October 2023

41635129R00071